Motocross

Kathy Galashan

Published in association with The Basic Skills Agency

Hodder & Stoughton

A MEMBER OF THE HODDER HEADLINE GROUP

Acknowledgements

Cover: Getty Images
Photos: All photos © Action-Plus Photographic.

With thanks to Guy at Motorcycle Action.

Orders: please contact Bookpoint Ltd, 130 Milton Park, Abingdon, Oxon OX14 4SB.
Telephone: (44) 01235 827720, Fax: (44) 01235 400454. Lines are open from 9.00–6.00,
Monday to Saturday, with a 24 hour message answering service. You can also order through
our website www.hodderheadline.co.uk

British Library Cataloguing in Publication Data
A catalogue record for this title is available from The British Library

ISBN 0 340 87700 6

First published 1999
This edition published 2003
Impression number   10 9 8 7 6 5 4 3 2 1
Year   2007 2006 2005 2004 2003

Typeset by Fakenham Photosetting Ltd, Fakenham, Norfolk.
Printed in Great Britain for Hodder & Stoughton Educational, a division of Hodder Headline,
338 Euston Road, London NW1 3BH by Bath Press Ltd, Bath.

Contents

1 What is Motocross?

Can you ride a bike?
Can you ride a bike
on a difficult, bumpy track?
Can you ride a bike
through the mud?
Do you like danger?
If you do
you might like motocross.

If you like danger, you might like motocross.

Motocross is racing bikes off the road.

It is scary.

It is dirty.

It is hard.

Riders follow a trail over hills and bumps.

They go through water at full speed.

They race on tracks with lots of tight turns.

They can race on sand or dirt.

2 The Bike

Motocross riders need a bike,
a special motocross bike.
Top makes include Honda, Yamaha,
Suzuki and Kawasaki.

A motocross bike is light and fast.
It has special wheels.
It has special shock absorbers
and suspension.
The tyres can grip the rough ground.
The shock absorbers and suspension move a lot
to give a safe ride.

The bikes are very high off the ground.
When a rider sits on the bike,
it sinks with his weight.

A motocross bike is high off the ground.

A motocross bike has lots of gears.
Low gears help the bike go up steep hills.
These bikes can go fast over rough ground
and they can fly through the air.

The tracks are bumpy.
When the rider hits the bumps,
he flies through the air.

3 The Clothes

Riders need special clothes.
They get very hot when they race.
They need a light shirt and trousers.
Riders need clothes
and body armour to keep them safe.
A rider wears a crash helmet.
He wears shoulder armour and a chest protector.
He needs back armour and hip armour.
He needs gloves, knee braces and boots.

Motocross riders need special clothes.

A good crash helmet is important.
It protects the head if there is a fall.
Riders need gloves to protect their hands
and boots to protect feet and ankles.
The boots have shin guards and side straps.
They have thick soles with metal tips.
Look at the rider going round a corner.
You can see that good boots are important.
All these clothes are very expensive.

Good boots are very important.

4 The Team; The Rider and The Mechanic

A good rider is brave.
He is daring.
He needs good balance
to control his bike well.
He uses his brakes well.
He uses the clutch
to control the gears.

A rider is one part of a team.
The bike is very important
as his life depends on the bike.
A mechanic is also part of the team.
He makes sure the bike works
and goes fast; very, very fast.
A mechanic tests the bike.
He checks the brakes, suspension,
the tyres and the engine.
The rider tells him what works best.
Together they check the bike
so it goes as fast as possible.
A good team wins races.

Motocross is a team sport.

5 Looking After the Bike

It is very important to look after the bike.
It must be cleaned after every ride.
Bikes get covered in mud and dust.
The chain must be oiled.
The air filter must be cleaned.

6 Races

Some races are for 125cc bikes.
Some races are for 250cc bikes.
There is a motocross Grand Prix.
In the Grand Prix
riders can enter any bike.

Big engines go faster.
But they are heavy.
They don't fly over bumps so easily.
They don't go round corners so easily.
Sometimes lighter, slower bikes win races.

The scrutineer checks the bike before a race.

7 A Day at the Races

The riders arrive in the morning.
Some race for fun.
Some race for money.
They are professional.
The bikes are checked.
The scrutineer checks the bikes
to make sure they are safe.

The riders are put into groups.
Then they all do a practice run
and start racing by midday.
There are 3 or 4 races.
and each race lasts 20 to 30 minutes.
The results of the 3 or 4 races
are added together
and the winner is the rider
with the most points.

The winner!

8 Jeremy McGrath – a Champion Rider

Jeremy McGrath is a rider.

He is a supercross champion.

He comes from Sun City, California.

Jeremy McGrath.

He started riding bikes
when he was two years old.
He used to play with the kids on his street.
The kids made up jumps
and he rode his bike over the jumps.
When he was 10 years old, he got a BMX.
When he was 14 years old,
he got a motorbike.
He practised on a private track
behind his house.

In 1989 he turned professional.
Professionals race for money.
Racing is their job.
It is a dangerous job.
Riders have accidents.
Once Jeremy raced with a broken leg
but he still won the championship!

In 1993 Jeremy entered a championship
with a 250cc Honda.
It was his first supercross championship
and he won.
In 1995 he won
the American Outdoor Racing series
and the Supercross Championship.
In 1998 he won again.
He become the most successful
supercross rider ever.

9 Finding Out More

If you want to find out
more about motocross –

– you can buy newspapers:
Motorcycle News.
– you can buy magazines:
Motocross Journal
Dirt Bike Rider
Trail Bike and Enduro Magazine.

10 Using the Internet

You can find out more about motocross
on the Internet.
If you are in the UK, search for this website:
www.motocross.com

Motocross Action
is an American magazine.
But you can look at the website
by searching for:
www.motocrossactionmag.com.

You can also search for this website:
http://trailrider.com/
This is Trail Rider Online.